LEARNING
to
TRUST
YOURSELF

LEARNING

to

TRUST

YOURSELF

*100 Encouraging Messages for
Growth and Healing*

Lisa Flannigan, PhD

LUMINARE PRESS
WWW.LUMINAREPRESS.COM

Luminare Press
442 Charnelton St.
Eugene, OR 97401
www.luminarepress.com

LCCN: 2019910999
ISBN: 978-1-64388-204-8

*This book is dedicated to the
beautiful wounded souls who,
despite their emotional scars,
have chosen to love.*

Acknowledgements

THIS BOOK WOULD not have been possible without love and support from some incredible people.

First, I want to thank my husband, Kris, who has always been there. You have been my rock. I am grateful for all the little ways you were there, such as making sure that I ate and rested and offering reassuring hugs.

I would like to acknowledge my first-born son, Nicholas. I am inspired by your hard-working attitude and the many life challenges you have managed while trying to stay positive.

I would also like to thank my daughters, Kelli and Emma, who share their playfulness, reminding me not to take myself so seriously. Kelli, thank you for being supportive, offering your artistic talents to promote this project on social media, and for taking the photo on the back cover. I am so grateful for all of your help while being a busy devoted mom. Emma, I appreciate you sharing your time and love for music with me. It has been inspirational and therapeutic through this process. Thank you both for your endless patience with my annoying questions and processing. You are amazing young women. My little ducklings all grown up, you are and always will be my heart.

Thank you to my son-in-law, Justin Loban. I am proud of the loving care you take of my daughter and grandchildren while you serve our country. This eases my anxieties knowing they have you.

I would like to acknowledge the inspiration and pure enjoyment that I receive from my grandchildren, Benjamin and Phoebe.

I would also like to acknowledge my soon-to-be daughter-in-law, Courtney Petty, for the warmth, patience, and grace you have demonstrated in this process of merging our families. I am grateful that Nick has you in his life.

Thank you Edward "Andy" Anderson for your support during a very tough time. Although we hit a wall that we could not get past, I am grateful for all that you gave.

Thank you Michael Freeman for your insightful support when my vision became dark. I am so grateful to have the opportunity to work with you.

Thank you Chris Elise for listening when I rambled on about one frustration after another while providing relaxing facials that are my favorite self-care rituals.

Thank you my dear friend Kelly Klippel, who, although too much time lapses between "our time," you have been a warm kindred spirit and sweet presence in my life.

Thank you Melinda Copp for your editorial guidance on a different book. Even though I learned a lot, I discovered it was not the book that I needed to write. Your encouragement helped me continue to write daily and to change projects. Thank you for referring me to Luminare Press. Maybe I will get back to writing that other book at another time.

I want to acknowledge and express my gratitude to the people at Luminare Press, who have made my ideas into a tangible book.

I would also like to sincerely thank all of the clients that I have seen in my practice, who trusted me with their private and painful experiences. You have all been a source of constant inspiration in your courage to work though life's challenges and hope for a more fulfilling life.

There are so many others that I would like to acknowledge who may not realize their positive influence in the writing of this book, such as my Instagram community: friends, family, followers, and those that I follow who offer bits of inspiration, hope, encouragement, and pictures of pets. I am so grateful.

Introduction

I HAVE WORKED AS a therapist for over thirty years. I have been inspired by people I have worked with that have survived many painful experiences but had the courage to hang on and create meaningful lives.

In addition, I have battled with my own inner darkness: traumas, insecurities, anxiety, and depression. In my struggles to work through the dark places and move to a place of healing, I have learned some valuable lessons. These thoughts have helped me and many of my clients over the years through painful times. I would like to share these with you.

I have come to understand that people in pain are only capable of taking in a little light at a time. In this book I have attempted to condense a healing thought into a simple digestible message. Each of you has an incredible life journey that only you can take.

This book is my gift to those who may be in pain, fighting darkness, feeling alone and disconnected from others and yet still courageous enough to hope for healing, peace, and joy in your life. It incorporates mindfulness, self-acceptance, setting personal boundaries, creating awareness and balance with your emotions, learning to trust yourself, and shifting self-defeating negativity to more growth focused optimism.

The best way to use this book is to reflect on one message a day or a week and allow it to teach you what it needs to. Since everyone is unique, each of you may take something that is important and meaningful to you and your life. Trust your own process.

This book is not a substitute for appropriate mental health treatment. My hope is that it can complement your work with a qualified mental health provider.

In addition, I believe that developing a daily practice of journaling, meditation, being in nature, and exercising are important for mental and physical health.

1

Take a moment throughout the day to just 'be.' Notice how you are feeling. Notice what you appreciate about right now. Joy is not about the big things. It is found in the little things like hearing the birds outside or seeing a tree with spring blossoms. Pay attention to what warms your heart in the small moments of your day, such as the taste of that first cup of coffee, the smell and feel of clean sheets at night, or the smile on the face of someone you care about. Drink in those beautiful seconds of bliss that together create an enchanted life.

2

It is OK to be happy and continue to grow even when people are suffering. Everyone is on their own journey. Sometimes, no matter how much you want to help, you cannot save someone from their own life experiences. It can be difficult to witness someone struggling. You may feel helpless and have empathy for their pain.

Although you may care deeply, you cannot rescue them because it is their life path, not yours. You can only support them with love, light, and acceptance and trust that they have the inner strength to overcome their challenges.

3

You are unique and beautiful. Please do not compare yourself to others. You are a rare and precious gem like no other. No one can ever be "you." What you have to offer is perfect. Your light is irreplaceable.

4

It is going to be OK. All your fear will be calmed and comforted. You are not alone in your suffering. People are there, and they care even if you cannot feel it right now. You are in the right place at the right time doing the right thing just for you. Sometimes growth and clarity are not in sync. Sometimes the reason for the pain or despair you may be feeling doesn't make any sense until later. You will look back and realize that you were doing exactly what you needed to do to get to where you needed to be. It is going to be OK.

5

Self-Acceptance is healthy. Accepting your strengths is valuable. It is also important to accept your limitations. You are doing the best you can in the moment, and that is enough.

6

You can relax, breathe, and take in this moment. There is enough time and space to accomplish what you want and need. You are brave enough. You have enough resources. You are attractive enough. You are strong enough. You are loved enough. You have enough to give because there is enough to go around.

7

Some days can be so challenging to face. Going through the steps of your morning routine and braving the tasks ahead of you will help you get into the flow of your life. On tough days you may not understand what you are learning or why you are going through so much pain. These days are merely about surviving and making extra time for self-care. Everyone has these days occasionally. Reward yourself for just getting through them. Self -understanding will come later. Just be gentle with yourself through each step, and remember that you are loved and deserving of tender care.

8

Being grateful is not about denying that you may be facing seemingly overwhelming challenges. It is allowing space in your mind to focus on those gifts in your life that you may forget to acknowledge. By doing so you can shift your energy and experience those good feelings inside just waiting for you to enjoy them.

9

Taking care of yourself and accepting your needs is crucial to your survival on this planet. It is not selfish to put your needs first before attending to others. It is impossible to take care of anyone else unless you are healthy and strong. Trying to save someone who pulls you down with them will only cause you both to drown.

10

It can be hard to watch someone struggle with their life challenges. You may feel pulled into their level of pain and lose your center. Remaining grounded in your life path can sometimes be difficult. You cannot be of help to anyone however if you are not self-aware and anchored in your own strength.

11

Grounding yourself in the present moment is the most efficient way to joy. Appreciating the input from all your senses (sight, smell, taste, sound, and touch) can remind you that now is perfect. This experience will never be here again. So, enjoy it, and take it in. Nothing is as important as this moment in time.

12

We all need reassurance every once in a while. Being reminded of our value in this world by others inspires us to live more thoughtfully and purposefully. Sometimes we can forget the positive impact our life has had on so many. Breathe, and take a moment to honor the very essence of who you are and how far you have come in your life.

13

Pain is, unfortunately, a part of life. It can teach us so many things. We can find our resilience when we face it and allow it to wash over us like a wave without telling ourselves negative beliefs about why we are suffering. Thoughts such as "I deserve this," or "I am meant to always suffer" are not helpful. Sometimes suffering becomes part of our identity, and it is hard to see that intense physical or emotional pain is temporary. Afterwards we are relieved and develop a deeper appreciation for peace and joy. It can teach us something about how we are living our lives but is not meant to 'become' our reality. When someone stays focused only on their pain, they lose the capacity to experience the other side that feels good. Respecting your pain yet leaving a space for healing will help you grow.

14

Create a safe space around yourself. Let in only those that treat you with respect. If someone continually cannot do so, they will only drain you and deplete your internal resources. This giving away of your time, attention, and energy is detrimental to your health. Communicate clearly how you need to be treated. This comes only from knowing yourself and what you need. You will probably reassess this often. Then, through your words, actions, and posture let people know who you are and what is OK with you and what is not.

15

Some days you may wonder what your life is all about. Do you have a purpose for being here? You may feel insignificant compared to greater humanity. On these days all you have to do is show up. Your part is an intricate thread in the tapestry of life. Your being adds texture to the overall pattern. So, know your value in this world. It is more important than you could ever have conceived. Just trust that your piece of the greater puzzle is crucial and necessary.

16

You are worth the time and effort it takes to be heard and understood. When you need to feel accepted and cared about, it is OK to ask for what you want from people that you trust. If they seem to be uninterested or distracted, that is not about you. Keep trying. Be clear. Do not expect people to read your mind just because they know you. Take the risk and be vulnerable because you are worth love and attention.

17

Sometimes you will feel anger: for feeling misunderstood, being taken advantage of, or by being treated poorly by someone. It is OK to have these feelings. They are valid even if not enjoyable. So, feel them and express them if you need to. Then let them go and move on. Staying immersed in those painful emotions harms your body and soul. Remember all of those things in your life that bring you joy. Relish all those moments that you cherish. Realize that usually the good does outweigh the bad. You, in your pain, have just forgotten the good for now. It is understandable. Just try to remind yourself these feelings are temporary and cannot erase all the gifts in your life.

18

You have to teach people how to teach you. Only you know the best way to be handled. If you feel that someone you care about is not able to support and care for you the way that you need, then you must tell them. If they cannot seem to hear you, give yourself some time and space to figure out what those barriers are. Are they incapable? Are they feeling inadequate? Do you both need help and guidance in your communication with one another?

Sometimes, and only rarely, it is time to let them go and be open to other relationships with people that are available to you.

19

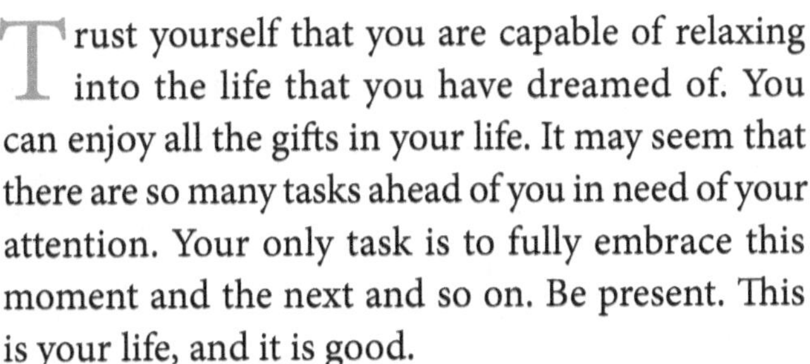

Trust yourself that you are capable of relaxing into the life that you have dreamed of. You can enjoy all the gifts in your life. It may seem that there are so many tasks ahead of you in need of your attention. Your only task is to fully embrace this moment and the next and so on. Be present. This is your life, and it is good.

20

On days that it is hard to move forward because you are feeling overwhelmed and are struggling to face the day, accept your feelings. They are not good or bad; they are just what you are feeling right now. Try not to judge them or yourself. Just let them be. Then focus on the next small step that you can take. You may find that you do not accomplish what you had hoped. However, you may find that you accomplish more. Reward your efforts with something nurturing.

21

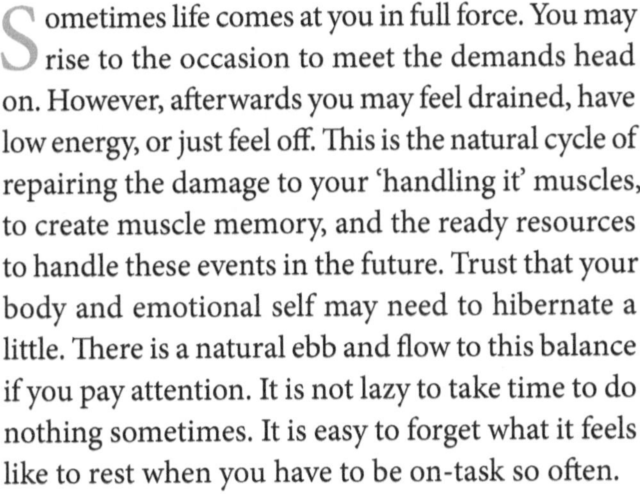

Sometimes life comes at you in full force. You may rise to the occasion to meet the demands head on. However, afterwards you may feel drained, have low energy, or just feel off. This is the natural cycle of repairing the damage to your 'handling it' muscles, to create muscle memory, and the ready resources to handle these events in the future. Trust that your body and emotional self may need to hibernate a little. There is a natural ebb and flow to this balance if you pay attention. It is not lazy to take time to do nothing sometimes. It is easy to forget what it feels like to rest when you have to be on-task so often.

22

Sometimes life is hard and confusing. You think you are on the right path for you, but obstacles or insecurities devastate you and seem to block the way forward. Trust that these hurdles will dissolve and work themselves out. You only need to stay centered in your sacred self. Eventually the road ahead will clear, and your next step will emerge and become obvious. It is going to be OK.

23

Setting boundaries with people is very important to your self-preservation. It can sometimes be uncomfortable to say no when there is so much pressure to comply. However, those feelings of discomfort and standing firm when you need to take care of yourself save you from later resentment and frustration. You get to choose where to set your boundaries because it is your life.

24

Trusting yourself can be difficult, particularly when you are faced with challenges in your life. Accept that you do not need to have all the answers right now. Allow them to unfold as you take the next brave step that seems right for you. Try not to overthink it. Step back a little, and remember to breathe. Then proceed with confidence knowing that your inner strength will be there for you whenever you need it. You have this.

25

I am sorry that sometimes you feel alone in your suffering. It may feel that when you really could use a friend, there is nobody to turn to. There are people who understand and have felt that way before. Everyone has moments of loneliness and despair. Do something to nurture yourself. Remind yourself that you are loved and worthy of care even if you do not feel that way right now.

26

Remember to pace yourself. Sometimes you may get so excited about a new venture that you jump in with passion and lose all boundaries. Being in this flow is wonderful. However, try to balance the energy that you are expending with peaceful moments of rest. This way you protect yourself from burning out and can enjoy your journey for the duration.

27

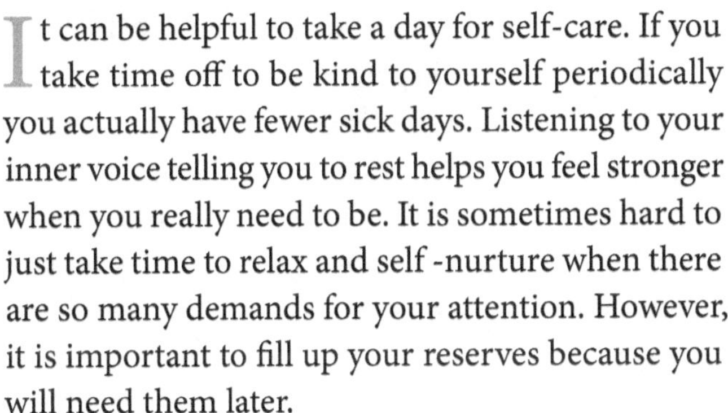

It can be helpful to take a day for self-care. If you take time off to be kind to yourself periodically you actually have fewer sick days. Listening to your inner voice telling you to rest helps you feel stronger when you really need to be. It is sometimes hard to just take time to relax and self -nurture when there are so many demands for your attention. However, it is important to fill up your reserves because you will need them later.

28

I know that some days you may feel rotten and wish you were someplace other than right here in your body. Just have a little faith that things will get better. Take note of how you are feeling. Acknowledge your internal experience even if unpleasant. Then slowly take a step into your day. If your discomfort eases and you get your momentum back, that is great. If not, just rest and allow healing to unfold. Your body knows what to do. Just trust it.

29

Things have a way of working out better than you could have imagined if you allow them to. It can be challenging to step back and breathe amidst stressful times. You may be tempted to immerse yourself in that turmoil. However, that energy could be better spent on restful creative tasks that revive you. If you put some plans into action, trust they will come to fruition in the best way for you.

30

Never lose your center no matter what life throws at you. Stay grounded in your own sacred space. It is your place of safety and security and is always there for you. Find comfort in the quiet calm of your own being.

31

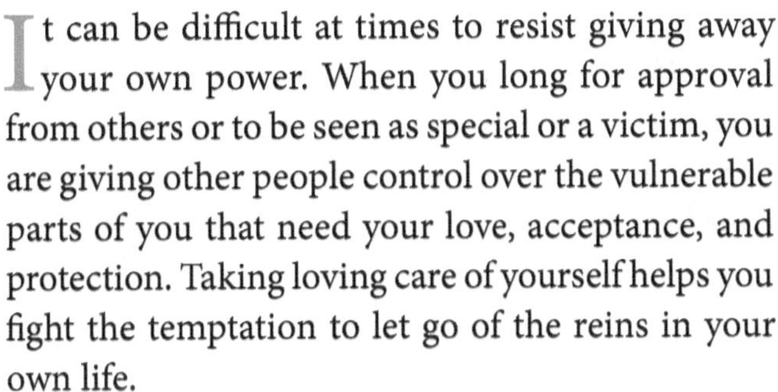

It can be difficult at times to resist giving away your own power. When you long for approval from others or to be seen as special or a victim, you are giving other people control over the vulnerable parts of you that need your love, acceptance, and protection. Taking loving care of yourself helps you fight the temptation to let go of the reins in your own life.

32

Everything is going to be OK. When you feel self-doubt or fear about the future you are forgetting that right now is good. Breathe in the peace of this moment. Experience your breath, and feel your heart beat. You will be OK.

33

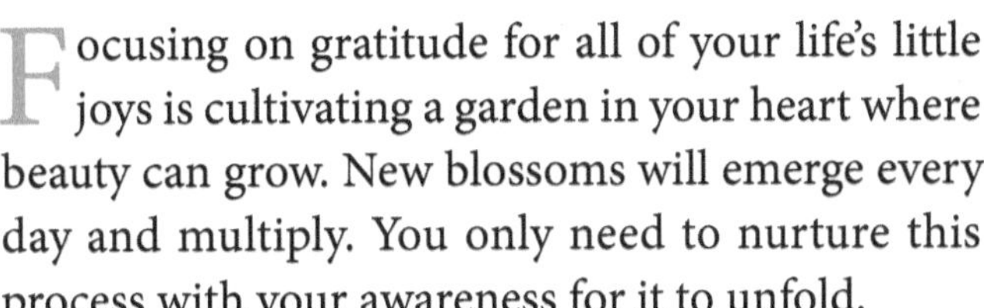

Focusing on gratitude for all of your life's little joys is cultivating a garden in your heart where beauty can grow. New blossoms will emerge every day and multiply. You only need to nurture this process with your awareness for it to unfold.

34

<hr>

Asking that other people treat you with respect and kindness is allowed. Just because someone is a family member or a friend or a professional does not give them the right to treat you with disrespect or cruelty. If you feel they do not have your best interests at heart they probably do not. Asserting that you would like to be spoken to and handled with dignity is an important way to claim your self-respect. Teaching people how to interact with you can be difficult for those of us who may have been abused. However, it is an essential part of healing and recovery.

35

Trusting yourself can be challenging at times. Sometimes it is difficult to trust that you are living your life in the best way for you. It is easy to look around at how other people are thriving and to feel either inadequate or competitive. It is not helpful to see yourself as lacking in comparison to others or to attempt to be better than them. What is important is to create your life the way that suits you. Allowing your unique path to unfold in front of you is a courageous act of faith.

36

Remember to take care of yourself. Sometimes, by staying continually busy, you inadvertently neglect listening to your inner voice. Try to pay attention to the wise, self-affirming voice inside, not the chattering, anxious inner dialogue. Tuning in to seek compassionate direction allows you to move forward with confidence and peace.

37

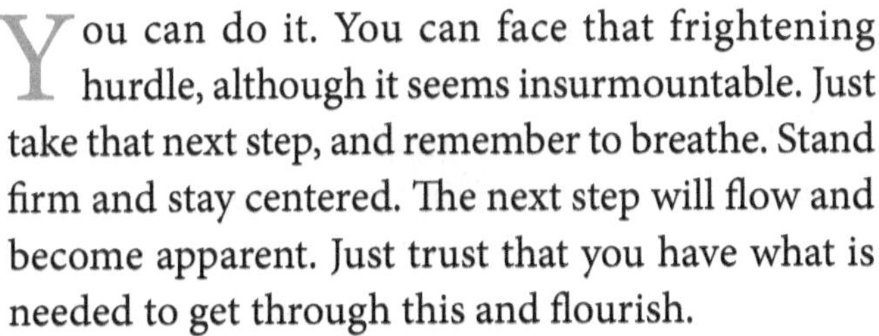

You can do it. You can face that frightening hurdle, although it seems insurmountable. Just take that next step, and remember to breathe. Stand firm and stay centered. The next step will flow and become apparent. Just trust that you have what is needed to get through this and flourish.

38

Acknowledge what you have struggled through and overcome. Sometimes it can be easy to lose confidence in your strength to face life's obstacles. In the midst of strategizing how to untangle your present challenge, you can easily lose sight of those skills that you have acquired along the way. You may forget that you have a tool to fix this problem. You only need to search your internal toolbox for it. It is within you. All you have to do is access it and apply.

39

There are going to be tough days. It may feel like you are being singled out to suffer, or that no one can understand what you are dealing with. Try to reach down deep and fight going to that negative space. Even if you can acknowledge one small positive joy, do that. These challenges will be over soon, and hanging on to your own inner light will make them less likely to stick around for long.

40

<hr>

Sometimes it may seem that you are completely alone in your suffering. Remember that you are not. Everyone has pain at times. You may feel that your struggles do not make sense and leave you completely confused. Things will be clearer later. Just keep trusting that the fog will lift, and your view will become clear again.

41

Please do not let other people tell you who you are. Only you can know that. Inform them who you are. Show them with your words, behavior, and attitude. Be clear because only you can paint the clear picture of you to show the world. So, own it, and present it. You are the original artist and author of your life.

42

Try not to be tempted to listen to other people's projections of you and what you need. Knowing what is best for you is your right. Trusting yourself is freedom. You are in the driver's seat in your own life. Backseat drivers are annoying.

43

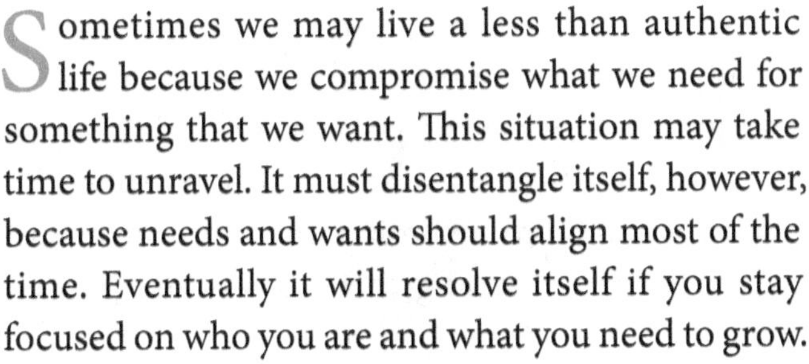

Sometimes we may live a less than authentic life because we compromise what we need for something that we want. This situation may take time to unravel. It must disentangle itself, however, because needs and wants should align most of the time. Eventually it will resolve itself if you stay focused on who you are and what you need to grow.

44

If you cannot accomplish all that you desire today, let that be OK. Give yourself acceptance and gratitude for what you can do today. There is always another day, and you will get there. Be patient when there are limitations. They can be just as much a part of your growth as your unopposed movement forward.

45

Feeling insecure sometimes is OK. Hopefully it does not last long. It can be a reminder to notice the strength and fortitude that you possess at other times. If you were not able to occasionally feel a little wobbly you could not appreciate when you are self-assured and solid. Eventually being grounded and secure will outweigh some passing shakiness.

46

Let the waves of emotion, oppression, or physical illness wash over you and return to their source. Do not allow them to become your focus. Yes, they may change you slightly. That is OK. You are not your illness, your emotions, or the oppression you have endured. You are, however, cleansed, polished, and made stronger as a result. So, do not get swept away with these waves. They will not last. Take note of the possible lessons you may be learning, and keep your attention on the enduring nature of your beautiful spirit that nothing can tarnish.

47

Discouragement is sometimes a part of life. It is not enjoyable but temporary. Sit with the feelings a little bit, and see if you can understand them. Timing may not be aligned for things to work out the way they need to. Taking a step back from the resistance is better than becoming enmeshed in it. This allows you a clearer view of the overall picture. All of the necessary parts will continue to fall into place eventually if you keep your focus on your hopes and dreams despite the challenges.

48

I deally, doing what you really love, no matter how trivial, helps other people. Engaging in joy-filled activities spreads that energy to the world. Interestingly, loving yourself and what you do is also loving others. You reflect light that attracts other people and becomes contagious. Find what brings you the most joy and do that.

49

Your path may be a little obscured right now. That does not indicate that it is the wrong way. It can just mean that something outside of your control has to happen first. So, try to be patient with your dreams. They are evolving like a beautiful butterfly. A lot of the work happens discreetly, as in the metamorphosis of the caterpillar hidden inside the cocoon.

50

Listen to this moment. It has the answers that you are looking for. Look underneath the distractions and the emotions to the quiet inner knowing. It is always there for you to bring you peace and comfort.

51

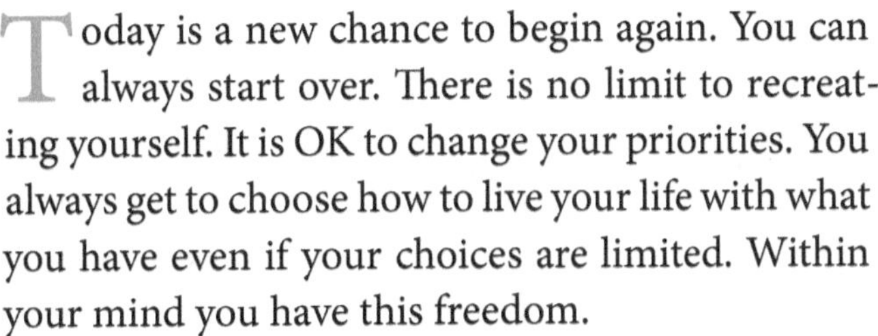

Today is a new chance to begin again. You can always start over. There is no limit to recreating yourself. It is OK to change your priorities. You always get to choose how to live your life with what you have even if your choices are limited. Within your mind you have this freedom.

52

Please try not to be discouraged when obstacles block your way forward. Focus on something else for a little while. It may just be time to rest and take care of yourself. Be patient; your path will clear soon. Obsessing about the hurdles is a waste of your energy. Save your resources for what is the best use of your time right now.

53

Even the little disappointments in life are gifts. It is when these challenges emerge and we can still find our center that we build internal strength. The only way to experience this power is by keeping our vessel afloat amidst stormy waters.

54

When you feel abandoned, choose not to abandon yourself. If you are feeling unlovable, love yourself completely. If you feel rejected, accept yourself fully. These are the moments that self-compassion is crucial.

55

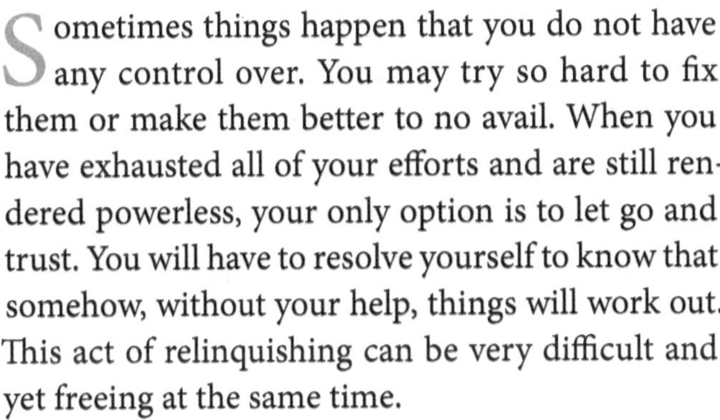

Sometimes things happen that you do not have any control over. You may try so hard to fix them or make them better to no avail. When you have exhausted all of your efforts and are still rendered powerless, your only option is to let go and trust. You will have to resolve yourself to know that somehow, without your help, things will work out. This act of relinquishing can be very difficult and yet freeing at the same time.

56

Staying grounded can be challenging when upsetting news tempts you to react negatively. Breathe in slowly, and remind yourself of how far you have come in your emotional growth. Under stress it is natural to regress a little, but try not to dwell on the negative feelings for too long. Reassure yourself, and be in your safe space until you feel peace again.

57

When someone you trust hurts your feelings, it can devastate you. Try to make sense of why it wounded you. Sit with your feelings, and try to understand them. If you care about maintaining the relationship, tell them they have upset you and how you would like to be treated. Often simple miscommunication can be easily remedied.

58

Feeling overly sensitive can seem like a handicap. It may actually be a gift. Accept that your feelings can be an important source of information for you. Learning about yourself and when to trust your emotions can guide you to your most authentic self.

59

Soak up the precious moments in your life. Let them resonate deep within your being. Feel the peaceful joy that accompanies them. These are your treasures that no one can rob you of but yourself. Guard them, and keep them safe within your heart.

60

You may not have a large group of friends. That is OK. You are still worthy of love and care. Just because you do not have a million followers on social media does not mean that you are not spectacular, valuable, and have a lot to offer this world. You may have a very small group of devoted people that you connect with deeply. Do not underestimate how impactful your life is on those around you. Your people may not be as present on social media, but they are still thankful that you are in their lives.

61

Try not to lose hope while facing a cold dark storm in your life. Hold on the best you can to the light in your soul even when it feels dim. The calm, fresh, and new always comes after the storm. With patience and letting go of the struggle, you can allow the needed transformation to unfold. It may seem like you are lost in the dark for a little while. Very soon the sun will emerge and you will see clearly again.

62

Why is it so hard to accept yourself with all of your human flaws and imperfections? Is it because you look to others to define who you are? You are different than other people, and that is OK and good. Being who you are is something that no one else can ever be. You may be surprised at how many people may view your imperfections as endearing and beautiful. Try to see yourself through the lens of affection and acceptance. Embrace the unique incredible being that you are.

63

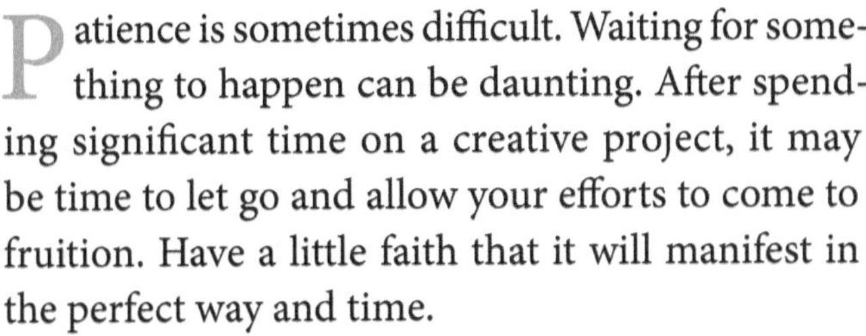

Patience is sometimes difficult. Waiting for something to happen can be daunting. After spending significant time on a creative project, it may be time to let go and allow your efforts to come to fruition. Have a little faith that it will manifest in the perfect way and time.

64

Some days you may feel as if you are not accomplishing anything. This can be frustrating. However, your mind may be unconsciously working on something that will manifest in the future while your body is relaxing. Lazy days are just as important as those filled with activity. Allowing your mind and body to rest helps them regenerate.

65

Trusting life and other people can sometimes feel impossible. Feeling safe and cared about is unfathomable, particularly if you have been hurt or traumatized by others. Learning to trust may be your greatest challenge. That is OK. You will get there. Focus on your breath and the rhythm of your heartbeat. You can find your center and courageously trust this moment and the next and so on.

66

When there are too many demands for your attention and your mind feels pulled in multiple directions, it is important to try to get out of your head for a little while. Go for a walk or do something else physical. Be mindful of the sights, sounds, and sensations as you move. Try to be present and experience your body, the rhythm of your movement, the feel of the sun on your shoulders, the smells in the air, the light through the trees, cars, birds, or people passing by. Your mind will clear itself. It will then be easier to return to mental tasks.

67

There is a synchronicity to your life. If you were more aware, these signs would be clear to you. Just know there is a larger manifest, and you are in the perfect place on your journey. Yours is a wonderful path. Enjoy it, and try to notice the miracles along the way.

68

꩜

When living your life feels daunting and more effort than ease, take a few moments to sink into your sacred center. Close your eyes, breathe fully and slowly, and let go of the outer world briefly. Let the stillness whisper a message of hope and encouragement. Listen to your heart. It is more real than the outer world. This is the core of who you are: perfect, calm, capable, and unlimited.

69

When you are overwhelmed with negative emotions, accept your feelings. By acknowledging them you discharge their intensity. Fighting against them amplifies their power. Telling yourself it is OK to feel this way allows the energy to move through you. This process allows healing and growth.

70

Sometimes you may make a mess of things. You may say or do the wrong thing, forget something important, eat too much junk food or drink, stay out too late, or spend too much money on something you don't need. There may be a dozen ways that you make frustrating mistakes. You are allowed to. You are human. Forgive yourself as many times as you need to. See yourself with compassionate eyes, especially when you have done something that you regret. This is when you really need your love and acceptance.

71

Focus on the gifts in your life. Even if, right now, they seem few. By paying attention to them, they will grow. Water them with your acknowledgement, and the garden of your soul will continue to burst into beautiful colors.

72

Holding on to your dreams despite adversity takes a lot of inner strength. Although at times you may become discouraged and feel your forward momentum is stalled, it is still within you. Try to be patient with life and yourself. It will happen for you.

73

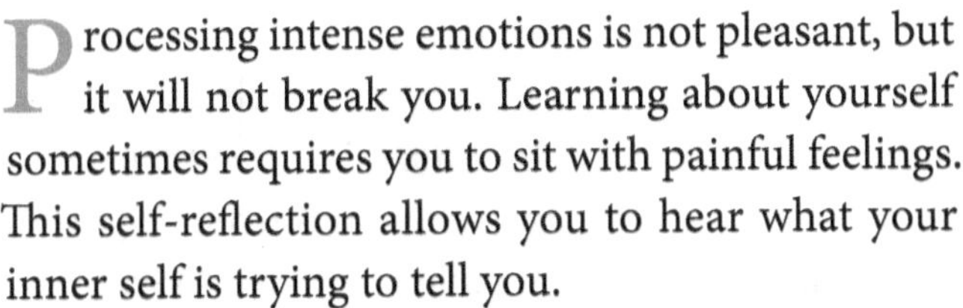

Processing intense emotions is not pleasant, but it will not break you. Learning about yourself sometimes requires you to sit with painful feelings. This self-reflection allows you to hear what your inner self is trying to tell you.

74

Feeling empty inside can be uncomfortable or even painful. You may be compelled to fill the space with noise and activity. Give it some time to see if it is just stillness inside. It may even become a peaceful surrender if you allow yourself to embrace it fully.

75

Experiencing rejection, criticism, or a verbal attack can be immensely painful. Trying to stay present and non-reactive is challenging. It is tempting to strike back and hurt that person as you are hurting. A more helpful response is to understand that the pain you feel is theirs. You do not have to take it in. Remind yourself that you are lovable, and release them to their own life lessons. Stay grounded in your beautiful light.

76

Trying to follow your heart when faced with opposition is challenging. Keep taking those small meaningful steps forward with quiet grace. Filter out the distractions, and stay tuned to the quiet guidance within. You know what you want, and where you are going. Stay centered, and you will get there.

77

Imagine an invisible shield of powerful light surrounding you. Feel this safety and protection providing you with nurturing and strength. Allow only loving energy to penetrate this armor. Create this boundary whenever you need to. Only you are in charge of it.

78

In each moment you choose where to put your focus. What you spend your energy on determines how you will feel. If you pay attention to the gift or value the lesson, you will feel positively. If, on the other hand, you perceive that something bad is happening, then a negative response will follow. It is important to remember that you get to choose.

79

⊸⊶⊷

Waiting for something that you desire can be challenging. Patience comes by accepting what is here in your life right now as you work toward your goals. Maybe the joy is in the journey, not in the destination.

80

Taking the next logical step in your life can be frightening. Trust that you are prepared. All of the time and energy that you have invested in this direction will pay off. Just breathe, and continue forward with momentum. This is where you need to be right now, enjoying the natural rewards of your efforts.

81

Courage can be difficult to rally when facing tough challenges. Sometimes it is a struggle to go through your day. Tackling small obstacles in your life, just outside your comfort zone, gives you the confidence to move forward. Honor these small acts of bravery, no matter how minimal they seem to others. You are building a repertoire of skills you can access at any time. These are yours, and no one can take them away from you.

82

⸎

Letting go of harshly judging yourself is a process. It can take time and practice to view yourself with accepting eyes. It is well worth it. When you create a compassionate inner voice, you will be more powerful than you have ever been. This support is always accessible when you need it.

83

Living a balanced life requires moments of solitude to listen to the whisper of your soul. It is easy to get distracted by external noise and lose your center. Breathe consciously, trying to stay present. This helps you remember what is important, and to let go of what is not.

84

Trying to untangle the thread of peace amidst surrounding chaos can seem impossible. All you have to do is follow it to its origin. Then bask in the warm embrace of stillness that awaits you.

85

Saying what you need to say can sometimes be frightening. However, it can be more painful to allow those unheard words to fester inside. Courageously expressing yourself may not only be cathartic but can forge a deeper connection to others.

86

It can be disheartening to long for something intensely from someone incapable of giving it. Accept their limitations, and know that your needs are OK. It may, however, be less painful to find other available resources to meet your needs.

87

Expressing yourself is OK. Some people will get you. Others will not. Do not judge yourself through other people's eyes. Allow your inner self to continue to emerge even if your first attempts are awkward. Communicating who you are will grow smoother with practice.

88

Painful experiences are temporary. Although they may feel endless, they are not. Try to hold on to the part of yourself that is strong, at peace, and feels like home. The discomfort is not where you live. That is why it is unpleasant. You are not supposed to stay there. Remind yourself there is peace beyond the horizon.

89

Focusing on achieving money, power, or social approval comes from feelings of inadequacy and a downward spiral of needing more. Knowing that you are enough and have enough leads to peace and joy. Believing in yourself and your competency will benefit you far greater than the need to constantly improve.

90

Let go of the focus on what is missing in your life. It leads to negative feelings. Pay attention to your gifts, assets, and blessings. Valuing the abundance in your life leads to fulfillment right now.

91

Trying to fill up the emptiness you feel inside reinforces your sense of deprivation. Stay in that space with acceptance and compassion. This slight shift in the moment can be powerful. Stay present with yourself instead of trying to be somewhere else. Right here in this moment, despite how you are feeling, everything is OK.

92

Who you are, at your core, is perfect. Forgive yourself for your shortcomings and the ways you feel you do not measure up. It is OK to be fallible and scarred. Being a fragile flawed human is beautiful. Embrace the awkwardness and the attempts to get up and try again. Just love, accept, and gracefully be you.

93

Loss is a part of life. It can burn and ache, but it is also part of the magical process of growth and evolution. Allow yourself to grieve the losses in your life. You will emerge stronger, more compassionate, and more beautiful than before. During the painful process it may feel like it is the end. It is, instead, a door you must walk through for a new beginning.

94

When there is too much noise in your mind to hear with your heart, breathe, let go, and trust. Your heartbeat will grow louder and clearer. It will guide you to your next step. Fall into the rhythm of your own life dance. It is one only you can perform.

95

Respect yourself when others do not. Have compassion for your struggles when others cannot. Realize your value when you do not feel it. These challenges may seem insurmountable. They, however, are necessary to own your creative power.

96

Sometimes everyone feels scattered or fragmented. It can be an uncomfortable experience. Being unsure of what you feel, what is important, and where to focus your energy can be frustrating. Just attend to the loudest demand first. The fog will gradually lift, and your next step will become clear.

97

Sometimes life seems unbearable. You may forget all the skills you have acquired over time and just feel overwhelmed. Remind yourself of the past hurdles you have conquered. You have what it takes to handle tomorrow's challenges. Just breathe and compassionately be there for yourself one moment at a time.

98

This is your life. You get to choose how you want to live it. No one can create it for you. Sometimes it may seem as though you are not in the driver's seat. It is easy to forget the choices you have made up to this point. However, it is never too late to make different decisions and to move in another direction.

99

Fear of failure can loom over you, preventing you from taking your next necessary step. Accept your imperfections, breathe, prepare, and venture out anyway. Bravely living your authentic life feels better than ruminating over all of the ways that you may not be successful. So what if you fall down flat on your face, and people point it out. You can cry or laugh, pick yourself up, and take another step. Reassure yourself, and take pride in your courage to try.

100

Taking that seemingly risky step that your heart calls for can be frightening. Trust yourself. That inner guidance is probably not going away. Maybe it is time to listen to it and move with confidence in that direction. You may fail. There may be roadblocks or detours. Just keep that momentum, and it will happen. This is your authentic self leading you to your beautiful life. Enjoy your journey.